Anupama Raju is a poet and literary journalist. Her poetry has been featured in several anthologies, including the *HarperCollins Book of English Poetry*, *The Yellow Nib Modern English Poetry by Indians* and *Prakriti*. Her writing has also appeared in *Poetry at Sangam*, *The Hindu*, *The Caravan*, *Indian Literature*, *Mint Lounge*, *Pratilipi* and *The Little Magazine*, amongst others. Anupama was the poet for a collaborative Indo-French Poetry and Photography Project (2011-2014). She is also a translator and has been translating Malayalam author Paul Zacharia's stories into English.

NINE

Anupama Raju

In association with the Jehangir Sabavala Foundation

SPEAKING TIGER PUBLISHING PVT. LTD
4381/4, Ansari Road, Daryaganj,
New Delhi–110002, India

Published in India by Speaking Tiger in hardback 2015

Copyright © Anupama Raju 2015

ISBN: 978-93-85288-75-3
eISBN: 978-93-85288-63-0

10 9 8 7 6 5 4 3 2 1

The moral right of the author has been asserted

Typeset in Requiem Regular by SÜRYA, New Delhi
Printed at Sanat Printers, Kundli

All rights reserved.
No part of this publication may be reproduced,
transmitted, or stored in a retrieval system, in any form or
by any means, electronic, mechanical, photocopying,
recording or otherwise, without the prior
permission of the publisher.

This book is sold subject to the condition that it shall not,
by way of trade or otherwise, be lent, resold, hired out,
or otherwise circulated, without the publisher's
prior consent, in any form of binding or cover
other than that in which it is published.

For Sankar

*'...brave love, dream
not of staunching such strict flame, but come,
lean to my wound; burn on, burn on.'*

—from *Firesong*, Sylvia Plath

THE NINTH LETTER OF THE ALPHABET: I

CONTENTS

No Borders	15
Poem for a Window	17
Name, Place, Animal, Thing	18
No Longer Mine	19
Monster Poem	20
On Borders	21
Voices Overheard on the Beach in the Minimes	23
Flying Home	26
On Seeing Sylvia Plath's Sketches	28
I Once Ate a Poem	29
In Chandni Chowk, Delhi	30
Chalai, Trivandrum	31
Mylapore, Chennai	32
The Temple of Tea	33
The Last Supper	35
Fatima Convent	36
A Universe of Uncles	37
No. 1, Bombay Flats	38
House of Dreams	39
Navaratna	40
For an Understanding God	41
A Folk Song	42
It Is a Poem that Brought Me to This Country	43
Stories	45

In Chiadzwa, Zimbabwe	46
Everyday Sounds	47
Between	48
The Memory Maker	49
Five Couplets for What Was	50
Disorient Express	51
Stories of the Dead	53
The Time-Eater	54
OCD	55
Eclipse	56
Sfumato	57
Tonight	58
Tale of a Forest	59
breathless	61
Love	62
Nightless Night	63
Disorientation	64
Black Horse	65
The Wait	67
Revolt	68
Born, Again	69

THE *NAVARASAS*

Sringaram–Love	73
Raudram–Anger	74
Bhibatsam–Disgust	75
Bhayanakam–Fear	76

Hasyam–Laughter	77
Adbhutam–Wonder	78
Karunyam–Compassion	79
Viram–Valour	80
Santam–Peace	81

I 82

No Borders

Poems sit on walls.
Moss-covered words fall gently
on my neighbour's page.

That yellow page has wings.
Van Gogh blue plumes fly across
seas named in old books.

I travel with those
books inside metal boxes
dancing on shy waves.

Waves lick distant shores,
land of a virgin language
looking for my tongue.

My tongue speaks mango
words, yellow with ripe meanings.
Drips into islands.

Islands float, brushing
against each other without
passports. No limits.

No limits here. Where
suns dip into syllables,
orange clouds hitch-hike.

Clouds, budget travellers
seeking summer tan under
sun-dried similes.

Similes wave from
a passing ship that sails to
those empty countries.

Empty countries wait.
Bowls that long for fish swimming
across language lakes.

I become a lake
but no lotus blooms in here
only poems of yore.

My poems sit on walls,
watch over neighbours, countries.
Poems have no borders.

Poem for a Window

We met a thousand years ago by a lonely window
I was a wild rose then growing by your window.

Forests of memories walk past greying cold doors
yet burning suns will always rise outside my window.

Lost scents hang lazily from an old heavy sky,
sting like rain on abandoned nights. Shut that window.

The wild rose forgets to bloom on still mornings
but birds remember my song roosting by the window.

Winds blow secrets from distant timid mountains,
bring back a country where I lived without windows.

A desert is born in dry hearts and thirsty minds
yet dreams feed on glowing sand, inviting like a window.

Words sleep like frightened children on dreary nights,
wake up as poems with wings. Open the window.

Name, Place, Animal, Thing

Letters stuck. Meanings
surge. Identities emerge.
What isn't in a name?

Poetry, Perfidy,
Porn—all things P. Pandora,
find us a place now!

Drunk-drift on four legs
seek attention, affection
from stray animals.

Touch, hold, smell, taste.
Made of memories and desires.
The thing is: I need.

No Longer Mine

Words fly without wings, hit against windows,
shattering glass, breaking into bits of fury.
Pick them up before it's too late,
glue them, quick.

Words swim without water, dribble down mouths
drowning voices, dissolving pauses.
Pull them out before it's too late,
warm them up, now.

But those words stand, mock, stare,
leave me behind, walk away.
Those words, no longer mine.

Monster Poem

Let me wake you up, creature of silence
breathe into your waiting body, feed you drops
of night blood so that you will survive the day.

You will survive, dearest spirit, in words
lying in cemeteries poets built long ago
to remember dead muses for centuries to come.

Your muse remembers you, beloved child of darkness,
as a brooding bundle of images, recalls how your five
limbs crawled into pages waiting to be stitched up.

I see you crawl now into this page, your ears alert
to the cries of a new born metaphor, your eyes
watching its fragile fingers curl into meanings.

But you are not fragile. A swift move and four stanzas
later, you swallow the unsuspecting ideas. Deed done,
greed fulfilled, you live again. While I die.

On Borders

Borders are like smiles:
Deceptive, transient lines,
sliding into lies.

Like the grains of sand
in distant deserts: flying
with winds. Homeless.

Like the songs of love
they once sang to each other:
Memories of pain.

Borders are like dreams.
Creeping into dark bed folds.
Real, not real enough.

Glass windows or walls—
never see them until too late.
Fragility lies.

Like spluttering streetlights
that live and die instantly.
Undependable.

Or like marriages,
devotion, dedication:
Conditions apply.

But not like shadows:
Alive at noon, dead at night.
They don't disappear.

Voices Overheard on the Beach in the Minimes

Shells will not do. Make
me a beach of your tanned skin.
I will not recede.

~

She seeks memories
of a sea in the waves. The
sand returns footprints.

~

Did you know, outside
your glass window the world's heart
bleaches into salt.

~

This sea smells of you.
Each time you drown it rises.
Give me back my sea. Live.

~

I walk on a stretch of light
where curt sand cuts swelling feet
and suns set in toe nails.

~

The lonely lighthouse
calls—seagulls and sails respond.
But this is not home.

'Voices Overheard on the Beach in the Minimes'
Photo by Pascal Bernard; from 'Surfaces and Depths'
(Surfaces et Profondeurs), an Indo-French photo-poetry
collaboration between Pascal Bernard and Anupama Raju.

Flying Home

I

Ten thousand eyes stare
as miles walk past
villages, faces, souvenirs.
A month of wine-dreams,
a mouthful of sin,
a lifetime of experiences
measured by each minute
breathe into me, in me.

II

Ten thousand eyes stare
as miles walk past
cafes, squares, museums.
Days of froth and freedom
a season of guilt
a summer of smells
folded into vanilla layers
melt into me, with me.

III

Ten thousand eyes stare
as miles walk past
terminals, boarding calls, transit halls.
Coffee hours of backaches
duty-free passion

stirred into wells
dig into me, away from me.

Countless journeys over
ten thousand eyes roll over
a death and a poem later,
I'm finally flying home.

On Seeing Sylvia Plath's Sketches

Sylvia, did your rooftops surface from
houses where poetry slept bored?
Your sweet things and insipid nothings,
your ubiquitous umbrella and the Beaujolais
your Paris, your Wisconsin, your Hawley
the absurd cow, the curious cat.
Did they all crawl into dawn
from the dusk of your words?
Did they float
with the lightness of your spirit
or drown
with you in interpretation?
Sylvia, take them back, back
to your scary metaphors
and fierce similes.
Your lines stay alive
in the night of your poems
not in the day of your sketches.

The Ubiquitous Umbrella is part of a collection of Sylvia Plath's drawings exhibited at London's Mayor Gallery in 2011.

I Once Ate a Poem

I once ate a poem,
it tasted of burnt letters
I wrote you in another life.
I once ate a poem,
it smelt of decayed words
I said when I was someone else.
I once ate a poem,
it cut like the knife
that sliced your heart out.
I once ate a poem,
it danced on my tongue
till I choked and spat it out.
Finally, the poem ate me.
Now I crouch inside it,
trapped in its meanings.

In Chandni Chowk, Delhi

Voluptuous markets
flaunt full-bodied wares of charm,
fragrant alley-dreams.

Goats chew on headlines,
grin ignorantly at fate:
Biriyani tomorrows.

Sunlight sleeps inside
attar bottles heavy with
the scent of history.

A b-grade movie
poster beckons near Red Fort—
'Loin Man' wins glances.

Biriyani: A rice dish cooked with spices and meat or vegetables; *Attar*: A natural perfume oil.

Chalai, Trivandrum

Incense sticks walk on
crowded pavements, mirrors float
in sandalwood clouds.

Flowers gossip past
grey chattering bicycles
that fight for space.

Step into puddles
of sweat, as coloured sodas
drown in arguments.

Turmeric noons blaze
as soaring appetites dance
in coconut oil.

Mylapore, Chennai

Fresh vegetables
and slush bathe inviting streets.
Fight with gods for space.

Oiled plaits, snakes charmed
by tunes of wayside flutes and
chattering bangles.

Eager nostrils take
adai-and-*avial* trails
to 'Karpagam Mess'.

Elegant silks dressed
up tall glass windows. I see
my wedding sari.

Adai: A savoury pancake made from rice and lentils; *Avial*: A dish popular in South India, made of vegetables and grated coconut.

The Temple of Tea

He makes tea for gods
with wisdom of the city,
devotion of a priest.
Works through steam
with clarity of the street,
vision of an oracle.
Pours the sun into glasses
with the benevolence of a tree
innocence of an infant.
He makes tea for gods
where his corner meets the world:
His tea stall, his temple.

'The Last Supper'
Photo by Pascal Bernard; from 'Surfaces and Depths'
(Surfaces et Profondeurs), an Indo-French photo-poetry
collaboration between Pascal Bernard and Anupama Raju.

The Last Supper

A couple sits at a bistro, their faces dark
from coffee. With every sip they draw blood,
with every bite they maul words.
By the end of the meal the sea would rise
and they would drink each other dry.

Fatima Convent

Buffaloes graze on
green memories that sprout
on my way to school.

Remember that shop?
Bottles of sinful syrup?
Fruit juice on credit?

The white blouse and green
skirt dry on the red terrace.
With them, my school days.

We went together
humming film songs, spilling smiles
till we reached school.

Yasmin, we rolled our socks down
to show our legs and
paid fines to nuns. Remember?

A Universe of Uncles

They arrive in hordes
of cigarette smoke,
laughing and swaying to
dancing bottles.
They roost in circles,
drowning gossip in folk tunes.
The frenzied moment comes,
packed in a plate of chicken
fried by hidden kitchens.
The evening ends in red eyes
and drunken snoring.
Morning arrives. Among glasses
and chicken bones, lie my celebrated uncles.

No. 1, Bombay Flats

Old doors wake up to a rusty doorbell
ringing, roaring, raving as I enter
a world lit by a sleepy bulb and a yellow wall.
Smell of fried fish, coconut oil, old books
sleeps in the apartment. Cobwebs hum.
Dust and dirt twirl in circles of silence
till a voice calls out from a chair,
where sits *Appoopan*, shining in his *mundu*
soaring, sparkling, spilling into my eyes
till I can no longer see him.
What remains is his smile.

Appoopan: 'Grandfather' in Malayalam; *Mundu*: A cotton garment worn around the waist by men in Kerala, India.

House of Dreams

I've heard it all before. A story of
wealth, fame, tradition,
brick, tiles, wood,
that went into ruin the year
I was born.
About the great Ambady *tharawad*.
'Oh, we're from the great Ambady,' *Ammoomma* said.
Ambady, whose ghosts still hover around Trichur's Elite Hotel.
Ambady, where prosperity once danced
where they grew up on *velyammoomma's chammanthi choru*.
Where happiness laughed at the doorstep
when suddenly teak doors closed
and opened to decades of bad fortune.
It's a family curse that ate into Ambady.
A parasite that fed on those prosperous times,
till the old matriarch crumbled under.
And history settled in, like fungus.
But the great Ambady still survives
in disillusioned, withering minds who still
know that musty feel, that woody smell of history.
And in me, as I dream
of Ambady, whose ghosts still hover around Trichur's Elite
Hotel.
Ambady, where prosperity once danced.

Tharawad: Ancestral home; *Ammoomma*: Grandmother; *Velyammoomma*: Great-grandmother; *Chammanthi choru*: Rice mixed with coconut chutney.

Navaratna

He wears nine planets
on ten fingers. One gem
short of good fortune.

Navaratna: A collection of nine gems believed to bring good fortune.

For an Understanding God

I slide in money.
Offerings for smiling deities:
Poorer by the coin

A prayer plays on lips
while my unfaithful mind drifts,
seeking his body.

When gods fall asleep,
my nights awaken from daze.
The sun can just wait.

A Folk Song

I was once your birthplace, your maternal village.
You grew as they fed my trees in this leafing village.

You built me a temple and invoked my blessing.
Did you know I'd bring rain to desert, my sleeping village?

The rain filled your stomach, you rose with water,
poured into an empty nest, your weeping village.

Floods came, you sang me songs, dried my tears,
but my rivers wouldn't nourish you seeping through the village.

You let go of my hand, cursed my love for you,
chose a new mother instead of me, your heaving village.

Summer's ripe with memories of you, my children,
but don't come back to me, to your seething village.

It Is a Poem that Brought Me to This Country

It is a poem that brought me to this country,
a map of rough words, a field of empty seeds.
The first line threw me into a well
of floating foetuses, limbs and two-finger test kits.
I could not breathe.

> *India is my country and all Indians are my brothers and sisters.*

The second line was kind, pulled me out
in a town where
trees waited for men
men waited for night
women gathered to fight.
I could not breathe.

> *I love my country and I am proud of its rich and varied heritage.*
> *I shall always strive to be worthy of it.*

The third line flew me over a village where
snakes drank white rivers
hissed at unfaithful gods
and babies slept rocking
to heady songs.
I could not sleep.

> *I shall give my parents, teachers and all elders respect*
> *and treat everyone with courtesy.*

The fourth line drove me to a mall
of glass fantasies, debris and discounts
where families shopped on delusional credit.
Money can buy you love, they said
as they dropped dead.
I did not say goodbye.

> *To my country and my people, I pledge my devotion.*
> *In their well-being and prosperity alone, lies my happiness.*

The fifth line alone knew where I could lie
so it took me to the city that was lost
to hired demonstrators, aging monarchs and migrant labourers.
It is a poem that brought me to this country:
a bench in Gandhi Park at East Fort.
I could finally die.

Stories

Ruins tell stories
of a child too, once playing
before her head rolled.

Heads rolled like teardrops,
settled amidst razed rubble.
Dried under dark suns.

Dark suns won't set. Days
freeze in smoky silences,
caught in still eyeballs.

Still eyeballs or bombs?
Toys of anaemic ideals,
but bloody war games.

In Chiadzwa, Zimbabwe

They wake up to eyes shut, cut
by bloody hands, lands, there
rough children sweat, shine, but
they wake up to eyes shut and cut
stone till it glows with white lust.
Country of a girl's best friend where
they wake up to eyes shut, cut.
A bloody hand lands there.

Everyday Sounds

The neighbour slams the door,
swearing at an unwelcome milkman
expects his next guest to arrive—
the other he would like to murder.

The lady upstairs grates a coconut,
drags a chair across the room,
hopes it will drown the argument
with the other whom she cannot hate.

The child downstairs wails,
holds a gun to her parent's head,
screaming for the brother's toy—
the other she wouldn't grow up with.

You chew weak tea without slurping,
read the papers, talk of the world's woes
in your succulent prose while I respond in insipid poetry—
the other language you don't acknowledge.

I continue to speak.

Between

The possibility of windows and the finality of walls
the irony of life and the innocence of death
the promise of soil and the treachery of sky
the humility of time and the arrogance of fortune
the rise of gods and the fall of faith
the excitement of hate and the ennui of love
the freedom of the road and the internment of destination
the lightness of mind and heaviness of feet
the unknown morning and the knowing night.
Between.

The Memory Maker

When she died
her body grew into walls.
Walls into feet.
Feet into rooms.
Rooms into eyes.
Eyes into roof.
Roof into hands.
Hands into pillars.
Pillars into head.
Head into cobwebs.
Cobwebs into hair.
Hair into air.
Air into dust.
And he turns
dust into memory.

Five Couplets for What Was

Fill the glass with shards of the past.
Do not drink, but learn to build from the past.

Memory is antidote to love, when the heart recalls.
Do not remember, turn away ill-willed from the past.

The body is a battlefield. Trading victory for identity.
Do not fight. Not with an army unskilled from the past.

Your photograph has started to bleed. Pour into old calendars.
Do not wipe, because it has spilled from the past.

Lips are sour. Wine turns to water. Water returns to tide.
Don't drown in it. Rise, unfulfilled from the past.

Disorient Express
For Irwin Allan Sealy

A train of thoughts
screeches past cities.
Crowded hearts, dreams,
lost compasses, drum beats,
smoke-lined eyes from skies
aboard a wagon, a grey
winding its way through greyed
pathways. Linger on thoughts
of clouds slipping off a sky.

Nightmares climb in from a city
seething amidst heartbeats.
Unwieldy passengers who dream
of homelands—dreamless,
dazed by fields that grey.
But to unheard beats,
moves the train, tunnels into thought
hiding under cities
safe from skies.

Carrying a skyful
of memories, sleeps in a dreamer's
eye, wakes up in his city's
embrace warm and woollen grey,
far from thoughts
limp under rain which beat
down windows of time. A beat

sends the travelling chorus skyward;
so proceeds the cortege—once thought
of as discovery of dreams.

But all that lies above is the grey
dust of former homes and forgotten cities.
Yet unmindful of spectres, our city's
gypsy carriage rattles along, beat.
Halts beckon, signboards invite. Greys
on to collide with sabre skies,
those swords of nature. Dreaming
tribes hop off the thought-train.

Journey ends, cities
come alive in the thoughts that beat
upon skies—rest in every man's dreams.

Stories of the Dead

The dead have a way with visitors.
Their eyes generous through tombstones
watch us pick our desired grave.

The dead have a way with words.
Their epitaphs shine with unfinished verse
read to us stories of love's lassitude.

The dead have a way with history.
Their cemeteries recall a city's lost life
restore the present back to its past.

The Time-Eater

He eats time because his bones will need memories
when they are stripped of flesh.

He eats time because whenever he opens his mouth
yesterday's profanity turns into today's poetry.

He eats time because his body is a clock
waiting to fill someone's tomorrow.

He eats time because his days shrivel into ants
gathering around dead conversations.

He eats time because his nights grow into snakes
slinking through aging loves.

He eats time because he needs to breathe:
Against the past, before time eats him.

OCD

For Inspiration through Deception

mind knows
heart denies
experience guides
memory misguides
eyes lose
dreams gain
body thins
skin thickens
hands allow
fingers forbid
feet stay
toes flee
lips move
words paralyse
language seeks
meanings hide
relationships die
obsessions survive

Eclipse

I shall not think of you these damned days
but let soaked silences thrive in rain
like moss-eaten lines brewing on my face.
I shall not think of you these damned days
but let moons swallow January sunrays
when diamonds of night shine, quite insane.
I shall not think of you these damned days
but let soaked silences thrive. Rain.

Sfumato

Was it silence that bleached
our conversation that day?
Forced its calm on us
as words lost their way?
We walked, I listened, waiting.
At the end of a tongue-tied mile
I thought there was a curve.
But Mona Lisa,
I knew I couldn't trust your smile.

Tonight

Tonight I will turn myself into a knife
cut into you for a glimpse of heart
just to know you are not dead.

Tonight I will turn myself into the body
you will not enter, you will not touch
just to let me know I am dead.

Tonight I will become the blood
that will scar this bed, this red. Love,
just to let us know we're dead.

Tale of a Forest

I

Love drinks me dry, yet I smell like rain
pungent wet earth almost washed away
by a passing storm that drifted lifeless
but lived in me long enough to die
quietly one day, leaving a seed here
a leaf there, a thinning forest.

II

No flowers bloom in this forest.
No. Yet I smell like ranting rain.
Lonely trees make their home in here
singing of a season not far away.
But do not trust spring, it too will die
quietly one day like words: lifeless.

III

Meanings lie cold—cobbles, lifeless
and lost in streams, once rivers in this forest.
Warriors of pain, they fight still, not willing to die.
Courage warms me, so I smell like the rain
pouring from eyes dreaming of loves far away
now dancing under a moon, afraid to rise here.

IV

Night swallowed the moon, spilling black here
but stars will always shine, smile. Never lifeless
is this kingdom, born to keep evil eyes away
but close to protect secrets of the forest
where I will always smell like the rain
where dreams shall breed, unwilling to die.

V

When dreams breed, desires don't die
but softly feed on the grass growing here,
grass that sprouts when I smell like the rain
and flow down hills, remembering a storm, lifeless
now breathing through hidden pathways of the forest
that shall never lead you home, too far away.

VI

Home was almost always far away
for many a traveller who came to die
in the lure of the fruit of my forest
that still hangs unplucked, untried here.
Fear not my gentle offerings, leave them not lifeless.
But taste me now, for I smell like the rain.

Thus speaks a voice not years away
from a rain that will die
when the storm leaves here, this aching forest.

breathless

the lights go out every time you pack your bag and leave my
heart when it beats
no longer to a melancholic drum but rests sinking in an
angry lake of *waywords*
that raise their beautiful heads refusing to drown in Time
who I don't wait for to heal
but drink from whenever I hide in her crevices that allow
me glimpses once
only mine now forbidden like the thoughts I was taught to
carefully despise but
I was never an obedient child so I empty myself of love
strip naked and swallow lust
till
I rise I rise I rise
and shine on the dark when the lights go out

Fits like a glove
Stings like a needle
Burns like a forest
Chips like a nail
Splits like firewood
Sings like the breeze
Turns like time
Drips like blood
Stings
Sings
Chips
Drips

Love

Nightless Night

Last night had no eyes, no ears,
no heart, no stomach, no skin, no bones,
no dark, no light, no spirit, no silence.
Last night had no warmth, no cold,
no pain, no lust, no gain.
But last night there was
a dream, a denouement, a door.
In the morning you were outside.

Disorientation

Blame it on the ocean,
on my frothing sea-breath,
on this opium air,
for all I can see now
are your plucked-out eyes
that continue to dream big
and become planets in your hands.

Black Horse

Cream walls float at an hourless hour.
Outside, the world's night is asleep
under a sky fixed like a stare
blue-black with beatings from dreams
floating on cream walls at an hourless hour.
Toss. Turn. Lie. Flat. Close. Open. Pillow burns.
Eyes gallop with nightmares that choke.
Pillow burns. Open. Close. Flat. Lie. Turn. Toss.
Nightmares close with lashes that stroke
cream walls floating at an hourless hour.
It is the nightless sleep of the mind
waiting to be awakened.

'The Wait'
Photos by Pascal Bernard; from 'A City, A Place, A Person'
(Une Ville, Un Lieu, Une Personne),
an Indo-French photo-poetry collaboration
between Pascal Bernard and Anupama Raju.

The Wait

You said you would come to me.
I danced on my terrace
till the sun dipped
till autumn eyes turned
to golden leaves and dripped.
You lied.

Revolt

Let me touch you,
endure the heat of the earth,
sear this lonely alley,
burn in the coal of your eyes,
melt in your hands.
Let us be on fire this night
as we scorch the city tonight.

Born, Again

Yesterday, I died:
In the teacup you broke,
spilling years of love.
In the letter you wrote
of a love once alive.
Yesterday I died:
In the green, green grass.
In the footsteps that measured
three and a thousand years.
Yesterday I died:
In the sliced onion
rotting in a dark kitchen.
In the lazy pile of dust
swept by wrinkly fingers.
Yesterday I died.
And today, in my place stands
a papery young rose
with dew on its petals
and the sun by its thorns.

THE *NAVARASAS*

Navarasas: Nine emotions usually captured in Indian classical dance or theatre forms.

Srĭngaram – Love

They scream, preach, scratch, score
in a ten-year old game played lame.
Sonnets go sour, ballads grate more:
Scream, preach, scratch, sore.
But when each day ends up as chore
or solace leaves suddenly as it came
he will dream, reach, search, soar
for her in the ten-year old game played tame.

Raudram — Anger

Hurl a bad poem at dawn
for destroying night's asylum,
demanding day's dignity. Spit, scorn,
hurl a screwed-up poem at dawn
for denuding secrets, leaving them torn.
Curse its sanity, bleed into delirium,
hurl a drunk poem at dawn
for destroying. Night is asylum.

Bhíbatsam – Disgust

This page reeks of rotten words
mouldy fingers, days-old sweat
stink of armpits, festering innards.
This page reeks of rotting words
bury it now with other things absurd:
Sting of logic, cold bite of regret.
This page reeks of rot in words
mould-and-finger days, old sweat.

Bhayanakam – Fear

One day the mirror will swallow
my head, your body, my hands, your touch
your bone, my skin, your today, my tomorrow.
One day the mirror will turn into a swallow
fly into my face, peck on my tongue's hollow.
Your blood, my nails, my wings, your clutch.
One day, I will mirror, will swallow
your head, my today. Your bone, my tomorrow.

Hasyam – Laughter

Orange trousers, blue belts and yellow shoes
Oily curls of hair, fee-fie-fo-fum muscles
daaarrrlings, good maaarnings, I lou yous
red shirts, bare chests and lovely see-throughs.
Come forth gods of yesteryears, sing to me
of Tollywood legends and the item number that sizzles:
Orange trousers, blue belts and yellow shoes
oiled skin so fair, those ghee-fie-fo-fum muscles.

Adbhutam – Wonder

Wonder letters, wonder fetters
Wonder sets you free. Wonder rise,
wonder fall: in your body, in your knee.
Wonder letter! Wonder fetter!
Wonder, come, fill me. Wonder shivers
wonder tickles, wonder fingers till she cries.
Wonder letters, wonder fetters,
wonder sets you free. One day, wonder dies.

Karunyam – Compassion

The world's kindest heart knows:
It is not easy to lend a beat;
let smiles reach where no one goes.
The world's kindest heart knows—
though loyalty meets cruelty, it grows,
if you give it all, much like Keats.
The world's kindest heart knows
lend easy, when loved, lived, beat.

Viram – Valour

He rose in gargantuan glory
tusk folding, forbearing, for getting
jibes and wounds quite gory.
He rose in gargantuan glory
over temple walls, miracle stories
to guard luck in the divine setting.
He rose in gargantuan glory
tusk forgiving, foreseeing, forgetting.

Santam – Peace

After the kill she lay tranquil
savouring stillness, white silence
hunger dissolving to fatigued will.
After the kill she lay tranquil
Sated blue belly spread uphill.
Sleeping soundly in nonchalance.
After the kill she lay. Tranquil,
savoured still. White, silenced.

I

My Englsh—
less
selfsh
tall
potent
more
snster
reverent
revocable
candescent
—wthout the
the nnth letter
of the alphabet

Acknowledgements

I am grateful to the editors of the following magazines and anthologies in which some of the poems in this collection have appeared:

The Hindu Literary Review, August 4, 2014: 'It is a Poem that Brought Me to This Country'.

Poetry at Sangam, June 2014: 'Disorient Express', 'Everyday Sounds', 'The Memory Maker', 'Five Couplets for What Was' and 'Nightless Night'.

Muse India, May-June Issue 2014: 'I Once Ate a Poem'.

The Caravan, November 2012: 'On Borders', 'Nightless Night', 'The Time-Eater' and 'The Memory Maker'.

Ten, The New Indian Poets, Nirala Publications, 2012, features 'No Borders', 'Tale of a Forest', 'No 1, Bombay Flats', 'House of Dreams' and 'Born Again'.

The HarperCollins Book of English Poetry, 2012: 'Monster Poem', 'Eclipse' and a version of 'Name, Place, Animal, Thing'.

The Yellow Nib Modern English Poetry by Indians, 2012: 'Monster Poem', 'Eclipse' and a version of 'Name, Place, Animal, Thing'

Pratilipi, January 2012: 'On Seeing Slyvia Plath's Sketches'.

The Caravan, July 2011: 'Poem for a Window'.

Mint Lounge, November 2010: 'A Folk Song'.

Indian Literature, Journal of Sahitya Akademi, May/June 2009: 'Tale of a Forest' and 'No Borders'.

Pratilipi, March 2009: 'Stories'.

Poetry With Prakriti, Prakriti Foundation, 2007-2008: 'Tale of a Forest', 'No Borders' and 'House of Dreams'.

Kritya, 2009: 'Born, Again' and 'No Borders'.

Mosaic, Unisun Publications, 2008: 'Born, Again'.

The Little Magazine, Vol IV, Issue 4, 2003: 'House of Dreams'.

'Voices Overheard on the Beach in the Minimes' and 'The Last Supper' were written as part of 'Surfaces and Depths', a poetry-photography project with Pascal Bernard, supported by Alliance Francaise de Trivandrum, Indian Council for Cultural Relations and Le Centre Intermondes, La Rochelle, France, 2014.

'The Temple of Tea', 'The Memory Maker', 'Stories of the Dead', 'Nightless Night', 'Disorientation', 'The Wait' and 'Revolt' were written as part of 'Une Ville, Un Lieu, Une Personne', a poetry-photography project with Pascal Bernard, supported by Alliance Francaise de Pondichery and Le Centre Intermondes, La Rochelle, France, 2012.

I am thankful for:

Initiation into poetry: The late Dr Ayyappa Paniker

Faith and opportunity: The Jehangir Sabavala Foundation, Ravi Singh and the team at Speaking Tiger

Support and belief: Arundhathi Subramaniam

Critique and confidence: Ranjit Hoskote and Jerry Pinto

Guidance: K. Satchidanandan

Encouragement: Antara Dev Sen, Rati Saxena, Priya Sarukkai Chabria, Adil Jussawalla, Paul Zacharia, Sudeep Sen

Freedom and understanding: UST Global

Collaboration: Pascal Bernard and Véronique Hirsche

Email conversations: Irwin Allan Sealy, Keki Daruwalla, Simon Armitage, José Marie Cortes

Comments and camaraderie: Karthika Nair

Friendship, warmth and warning signs: Swarup B. R.

Affection and humour: Saju maman

I thank my late grandparents whom I will always cherish. And my family, especially my mother and brother; and parents-in-law—the best parents ever.

And to Sankar who stands by me always: Thank you.

www.ingramcontent.com/pod-product-compliance
Lightning Source LLC
Chambersburg PA
CBHW052053220426
43663CB00012B/2552